IMAGES OF ENGLAND

AROUND
WHEATLEY HILL

IMAGES OF ENGLAND

AROUND
WHEATLEY HILL

WHEATLEY HILL HISTORY CLUB

TEMPUS

First published 2007

Tempus Publishing Limited
The Mill, Brimscombe Port,
Stroud, Gloucestershire, GL5 2QG
www.tempus-publishing.com

British Library Cataloguing in Publication Data.
A catalogue record for this book is available from the British Library.

ISBN 978 0 7524 4362 1

Typesetting and origination by Tempus Publishing Limited.
Printed in Great Britain.

Contents

	Acknowledgements	6
	Introduction	7
one	Wheatley Hill	9
two	Thornley	45
three	Wingate	79
four	Ludworth	115

Acknowledgements

The images in this book came from the following sources:

Wheatley Hill: David Atkin, Fred Bromilow, Wheatley Hill History Club.

Thornley: David Atkin, Fred Bromilow, Bill Middleton, Owen Rowland, Wheatley Hill History Club.

Wingate: Jack and Lena Devine, Margaret Hedley, Bill Middleton, Wingate Local History Group.

Ludworth: Fred Bromilow, Andria Ditchburn, Margaret Hedley, Bill Middleton, John Milburn, Owen Rowland, Wheatley Hill History Club.

The Ariel images in this publication have been included with the kind permission of Nostalg-Air and copies can be obtained by contacting: 0113 2811043.

We would like to thank anyone else who has loaned photographs – we are very grateful for your contribution.

Introduction

The villages of Wheatley Hill, Wingate, Thornley and Ludworth all came to prominence during the Victorian coal-mining boom of the early 1800s. Until then, all had been agricultural communities in the East Durham area. Formerly land-locked areas, the railways made coal mining possible in all four of these villages and thriving communities grew up around the pit heads.

Apart from the farms which still existed in all of the villages, the pit became the major employer and apart from the personnel needed to run shops, schools, police stations, public houses, etc., all men worked at the coal mine. Except for domestic service, occasional agricultural labouring, dressmaking and perhaps a small number of teaching jobs, there was little opportunity for formal, paid employment for women in the early colliery villages.

Alongside the collieries and associated housing, other amenities developed to support the miners and their families. Schools, places of worship, shops, public houses, etc., all sprung up in these four villages, which, in the early days of their coal mines, and before an adequate road or public transport system, were difficult to reach from the towns of Durham, Hartlepool and Sunderland, making the villages quite isolated.

The early villages were functional. They contained poor quality housing, unmade up streets, no drainage or running water and the stereotype of these settlements was one of dreariness and depression by outsiders not familiar with mining communities. The hastily built houses were always built near to the pit head which made keeping them clean a continuous battle for miners' wives. Access to the cottages was directly from a dirt-track into the parlour/bedroom at the front.

However, the inside of many of these homes was in stark contrast to their outside appearance. The pitmen of the Durham coalfield possessed furniture which was generally better than the dwellings they lived in. The interiors have been described as 'showy', with possessions such as an 'eight-day-clock', a good chest of drawers and a four-post bedstead. The miners' wives worked very hard to create a cosy, comfortable and attractive, homely interior, which was very difficult given the domestic disruption of multiple shift-working.

As the area developed throughout the early 1800s and became criss-crossed with roads, wagonways and eventually railways, the Durham coalfield had one of the earliest and most developed transport systems in the country. As a result of this, the area sustained high levels of local immigration, with miners and their families moving each year to look for a better deal from the mine owners (the moves usually taking place in April when their Bond was due for renewal) and it was common to see carts loaded with possessions travelling from village to village.

For all the dirt, poor living conditions, dangerous working conditions, etc., that the miners and their wives suffered, they were able to create real 'communities' which were supportive of one another, and there was a sense of belonging. At times of industrial unrest the miners and their wives in these four villages provided a united front against the mine owners – they knew what it was like to suffer hardship and would help any family who was in need, even though they had nothing themselves.

Unfortunately, from the 1960s coal mining began to decline in the East Durham area and with the closure of the mines, and the loss of its major employer, began the steady decline of the villages. People moved away from these villages, many to remain in the coal-mining industry in other parts of the country, others to look for new opportunities. This migration and the lack of a main employer in the villages led inevitably to a decline in services, an ageing population and lack of local opportunities for young people.

Over recent years, and with a desire to look back into their past, these four communities have been involved in charting their industrial history and building up an archive of material with which to educate future generations about the pride of their ancestors – the men who worked in the pits and the women who supported them. This publication provides a vital tool in that educational process and will hopefully demonstrate the closeness of the communities and the immense pride with which they are remembered.

Margaret Hedley
Wheatley Hill History Club

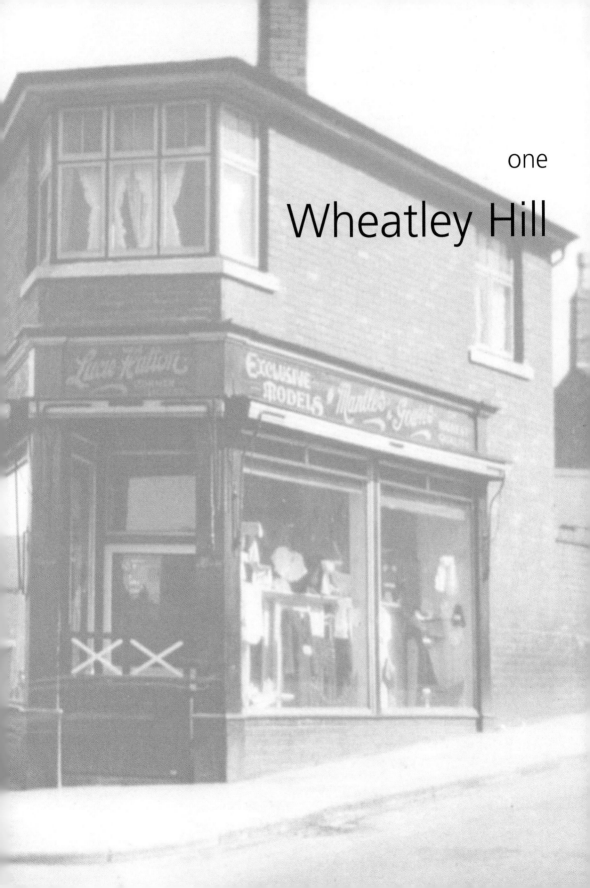

one

Wheatley Hill

Above: Rock Farm is the oldest building in the village of Wheatley Hill. Robert Rhodes inherited the estate containing Rock Farm in 1451 from his wife, Joan Hardwike of Little Eden. There is little doubt that at that time, Rock Farm was a manor house and given its age, it is of great architectural interest in the area. This image shows the farm as it is today. Despite its architectural treasures which have been uncovered over recent years, the building failed to be listed in the *Pevsner Architectural Guide*, probably as a result of the lack of written information about the original building and also the alterations made to 'modernise' it over the years which covered up its treasures until a major renovation programme during the 1990s.

Left: This image shows a doorway into the parlour dating from 1500. The top of the arch was removed at some stage but was sympathetically restored during a subsequent renovation. In the opinion of Peter Ryder, archaeologist, this was a superior doorway for a small manor house and must have been built by a wealthy family. It is more in keeping with church architecture.

Right: This image shows mason's marks on the side of the mullioned window in the upper chamber. Although there is no evidence to confirm this, Bishops masons who worked on Durham Cathedral may have been employed by the builder of the house, Richard Bainbridge, in the fifteenth century. He was a leading figure in County Durham, having been sworn in as a Commissioner of the Peace at Durham Quarter Sessions in 1471.

Below: This 8ft inglenook fireplace was uncovered during renovation work in the 1990s. Successive generations had built fireplaces inside the inglenook thus preserving the original fireplace.

The doorway shown in this image leads to the heck passage which allowed access into the hall from the kitchen area. To the left of the picture is the inglenook fireplace and on the right of the heck passage the remains of a stone spiral staircase can be seen.

This photograph probably dates from the early 1890s and shows Wheatley Hill Front Street, or High Wheatley Hill, or even simply 'The Farm', as it was known in the early days of the village. The area was known as The Farm as a result of Rock Farm being the only buildings in this area before the buildings in this image appeared.

This is another early image of Wheatley Hill Front Street showing The Nimmo Hotel on the right. The Nimmo Hotel was opened in 1874 and was named after the brewery that owned it – J. Nimmo & Sons of Castle Eden.

This much later image of Front Street was probably taken in the 1940s and shows that electricity had arrived in the village and motor vehicles! The footpaths and road are a welcome addition to conditions too.

The main industry in Wheatley Hill between 1868 and 1968 was the colliery. Before nationalisation the pit was owned by the Weardale Steel, Coal & Coke Co. This view shows the lamp cabin with Fred Armstrong and Tommy Mason.

A group of miners at Wheatley Hill Pit in the 1920s. In the back row in the middle is Mr Henderson and on the far right, Mr McKeand. Sitting in the front row second from the left is Mr Thornton, third from the left Mr Wilson and second on the right Mr Gair.

**"STAGSHAW" working at Wheatley Hill Colliery on 28th April, 1968.
The yellow liverytakes the fancy of some and was loathed by others.**

This engine was a common sight running between Wheatley Hill and Thornley collieries. Its formal name was 'Stagshaw' but it was known locally as 'The Tanky'.

A view of Wheatley Hill Pit.

Landing and loading point underground at Wheatley Hill Colliery in the 1950s. The loader head is on the left in the background.

Wheatley Hill pit yard.

Above: At the time of the 1926 strike, soup kitchens were a common sight in the colliery villages – this image shows canteen workers outside the Miners' Hall. In the back row, left to right: Mr Smith, Mr Havelock, Mr Galley, Mr Hird, Mr Havelock and Mr E. Cain. Middle row: Mrs Parnham, Miss Summers, Miss Summer, -?-. Front row: Stan Parnham, W. Turnbull, B. Venables and Tommy Venables.

Right: A pay note for the week ending 8 May 1943 at Wheatley Hill Pit belonging to Mr R. Gregory, who earned £5 0s 2d for working seven eight-hour shifts.

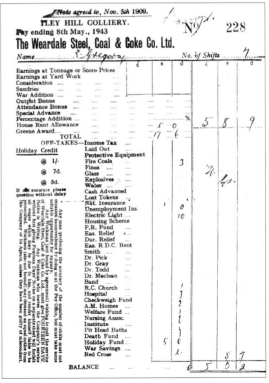

Every colliery village was proud of its brass band. This photograph was probably taken on the day of
the opening of the new Miners' Hall in Patton Street in 1910 when the band, with the colliery banner,
paraded through the streets of the village before attending the opening ceremony. The photograph
includes Jackie Lewis, Tommy Philips, R. W. Thornton, Teddy Kitto, Mr Matthew Barrass (colliery
manager) and Frank Quinn.

Opening of the new Miners' Hall in Patton Street – September 1910. The opening ceremony was preceded
by the band and banner being paraded through the village. The opening ceremony was performed by Mr
Michael Lamb, Lodge President. Tea, provided by the miners' wives, was served in the hall.

A 1940s photograph of Wheatley Hill Colliery Band taken outside The New Tavern public house situated in Wingate Lane, Wheatley Hill.

Wheatley Hill Colliery Lodge Banner 1998 shows Miners' Leader Peter Lee. Peter was born into a mining family in 1864 and went on to become checkweighman at Wheatley Hill Pit in 1902. In 1903 he was elected to the Parish Council. Peter was responsible for bringing about significant improvements in the village. The road to connect Wheatley Hill and Thornley, a cemetery and chapel of rest, a sewerage and water system and street lighting can all be attributed to his efforts. He was also a lay preacher at the Primitive Methodist church in Patton Street. In 1919 Peter Lee became the chairman of Durham County Council, the first labour-controlled county council in this country – and Peter was its first chairman.

The first Wheatley Hill 'Workmen's Club' opened in 1904 in an area known locally as 'over the beck'. There had been much opposition to the opening of a working men's club, especially from the coal owners who felt that if men were spending time drinking it would affect their attendance at work.

Despite opposition from the coal owners the club was a thriving enterprise – this image shows the Darts and Dominoes Club in 1930 (Mr Burnside, Mr Redshaw, Mr Prior and Mr Dunn, the treasurer). The gentleman on the right is holding a Club & Institute news-sheet in his hand.

This is the Colliery Hotel which was also situated 'over the beck' at the end of Lynn Terrace. The pub was built in the 1870s and the houses in the 1890s. This public house was owned by Mr Binks from Thornley.

This is the first Wingate Tavern situated in Wingate Lane, Wheatley Hill on the opposite side of the road to the New Tavern which opened in the 1940s. The Wingate Tavern is now the premises of the Wingate Lane post office.

The Primitive Methodist chapel, Patton Street was the oldest religious building in the village. It re-opened in 1898 after extensive alterations. Sadly, as a result of a deteriorating building, the Primitive Methodists stopped holding services in the building during 2004. However the building was taken over by a group of Evangelists who were able to make improvements to it and now hold their services there.

All Saints church, Wheatley Hill was built in 1912 as a result of the villagers raising money to build a church, church hall and vicarage. The church contains a tablet and pipe organ to the memory of those who lost their lives during the First World War.

The Wesleyan Methodists were also active in Wheatley Hill at the end of the 1800s and the beginning of the 1900s. This image shows a group of people from the Wesleyan chapel possibly at the time of their anniversary when they carried their musical instruments around the streets of the village, stopping to play hymns at various points. Before they had an official building, this group met in a house provided by the colliery owners, in Ford Street.

The Cemetery, Wheatley Hill. 5844

Wheatley Hill cemetery opened in 1907 after much canvassing by the chairman of the Wingate parish council, Mr Peter Lee. Wheatley Hill came under the auspices of Wingate parish council until 1974.

This was the first school built in Wheatley Hill in about 1873, just after the 1870 Act which made education compulsory for all children. Over the years it served as an infant, junior and senior school and in its later years as the Senior Boys School. The building no longer exists and pupils of secondary age now travel to Wingate, Peterlee or Durham.

Cookery class at Wheatley Hill Senior School in the 1930s. The recipe on the blackboard is for 'Ground Rice Mould'. The girls would have been expected to make their caps and aprons during sewing lessons.

Class 4 at Wheatley Hill Junior School, 1927.

In October, 1938 a new secondary school for girls opened in Wordsworth Avenue. It was named Peter Lee Secondary School in memory of the man who had done so much for the village of Wheatley Hill. At the time of opening, the school provided girls with a gymnasium, showers, two purpose-built home economics rooms and seven teaching classrooms. The school could cater for educating 360 girls aged eleven to fourteen.

This group of boys from Wheatley Hill Senior Boys School were 'Digging for Victory'. Under the guidance of their head teacher, Mr Arnold, they dug and set the gardens belonging to elderly people in the village in order to provide them with vegetables during the Second World War. Back row, left to right: Robert Taylorson, Freddy Ward, Maurice Wharrior, Russell Lake, Harry Eddy. Middle row: Freddy Peacock, Mattie Hanley, Gordon Carr. Front row: Tommy Hedley and Kenny Kendal.

Right: School Report of Ruth Horan, a pupil at Wheatley Hill Infants School in 1926.

Below: A group of pupils at Wheatley Hill Primary School in 1947. Back row, left to right: Eric Cockburn, Billy Ord, Tommy Durant, Billy Walker, Keith Johnson, Ray Galley, Tom Walker, Morris Nicholls. Middle row: Gladys Raine, Freda Scott, Margaret Camiss, Jean Armstrong, Yvonne Dodds, Judith Grey, Margaret Young. Front row: Irene Binks, Dorothy Powell, Ella Lee, Muriel Ferry, Jean Jobes, Sonia Vincent, Margaret Carter, Ann Smith, Isabel Howarth.

Opposite below: This 1948 photograph shows the staff at Wheatley Hill Infants School. Back row, left to right: Mrs Graves, Mrs J. Smith, Miss S. Lee *(granddaughter of Peter Lee)*, Mrs O'Connor, Mrs Atkinson, Margaret Brown (school clerk). Front row: Mrs Wardell, Mrs Hunter, Miss Bellinger, (head teacher), Mrs Charlton and Miss Cruttenden.

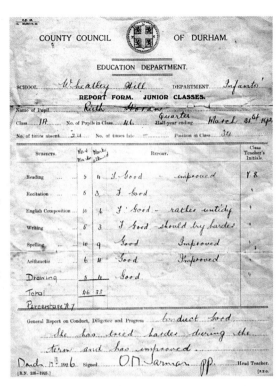

Winners of the Baldasera Cup at Wheatley Hill Primary School, 1957. Back row, left to right: Mr Willan (head teacher), W. Cowey, D. Hoole, J. Wynn, J. Tempest, W. Howarth, D. Metcalfe, Mr Lister. Front row: S. Burdett, L. Jones, W. Gibson, W. Halliwell, J. Lowther, O. Rowland.

'It's Good, It's Baldasera's', became a well-known slogan in the colliery villages around Wheatley Hill as a result of Angelo Baldasera, who set up business in Thornley early in the 1900s. He extended his shops to Wheatley Hill and Shotton Colliery and his ice-cream cart was a familiar site in all surrounding villages.

Nixon Bros was a familiar sight in the village in the early 1900s. The Nixon family were originally from the East Cleveland area and it is not clear how they came to open a shop in Wheatley Hill, but as can be seen from the photograph, it was a substantial business. It stood on the site which later became the store garage.

A familiar sight throughout the colliery villages was that of Walter Willson's grocery shops, which promised 'A Smiling Service'. This particular branch was at the top of Church Street, Wheatley Hill.

Above: A 1960s image of Fletcher's butchers shop in Granville Terrace (once known as Front Street). The premises, after some alterations, remained a butcher's shop until 2006.

Left: This is Sally Smiles with her caravan where she sold sweets during the 1930s. The caravan was situated in the colliery rows near to Elizabeth Street.

A shop selling quality clothing for women and children is still remembered today as Lucie Hutton's.

Smart Seasonable Wear

——————for Indoors and Out——————

DRESSES, GOWNS, COSTUMES, COATS, Etc.

The Newest and most Exclusive of the Season's Productions always in Stock

Agent for "Portland" Shoes and "Bear Brand" Hosiery

LUCIE HUTTON

Hosiery and Lingerie Specialist

Corner House, WHEATLEY HILL

Wrapping paper used by Lucie Hutton's shop.

Above: The Co-operative Wholesale Society (CWS) was a very popular shop throughout the colliery villages and was known as 'the store'. This image shows Billy Natrass with his store horse in 1949. The store horses and carts made deliveries of groceries door to door around the village

Opposite below: The Sherburn Hill CWS opened a branch in Wheatley Hill in March 1912. The store had a café when it first opened and an Italian roof café was planned for later development. Unfortunately, that never came about. This image shows staff on the baby linen counter in the 1950s: Margaret Jones, Betty O'Connor, Maureen Craven and Valerie Smith.

Right: When catering for weddings was done by the bride's parents, most of the food would be bought from the store in order to collect the dividend that such a large order would attract. This is a shopping list for a 1939 wedding.

Below: The grocery department in Wheatley Hill Co-operative (the store). The members of staff in the picture are A. Bishop and W. Armstrong and the customer is Mrs Maddison.

BRANCHES:
Sherburn, Shotton, Wheatley Hill, Horden.

May 23 193 9

M W Rare. -

BOUGHT OF THE

SHERBURN HILL CO-OPERATIVE PROVISION SOCIETY

LIMITED.

The Palace Theatre opened in October 1913 in Wheatley Hill Front Street, near The Nimmo Hotel. Mr James Porter was the first manager and he reported packed houses during the first few months after opening.

After a refurbishment, The Palace Theatre reopened as The Royalty Cinema in December 1938. It was a typical 1930s art-deco building.

The foyer of The Royalty after refurbishment in 1938.

The Royalty were advertising widely across the village with their new vehicle parked outside the colliery offices where it would attract the attention of men working at the pit.

View of the pit from the cricket field area in the early 1960s.

In June 1928 a bowling green was an added attraction to the Miners' Welfare Park in Wheatley Hill. The green was in addition to five tennis courts, a croquet green, an extensive children's playground and a band stand.

In addition to the magnificent facilities provided in the Miners' Welfare Park, a sports and dance centre was added in 1931. The building cost £4,250 to build and this money was raised from the penny-a-ton fund set up at the colliery when a penny for every ton of coal was paid into a building fund by the coal owners.

Wheatley Hill Institute, winners of the Houghton & District Billiard League, 1912-13. Back row, left to right: R. Hird (treasurer), A. Turner (secretary), W. Jones, W. Lamb, S. Dickinson. Front row: T.M. Robinson, W. Greenwood, R. Winter (Pitman's Champion 1913), T. Hird.

Wheatley Hill Football Team, 1912. Back row, left to right: W. Halsall, W. Jackson, J. Craig, G. Robinson, E. Cain, W. Ward, S. Briggs, L. French, A. Turner. Middle row: B. Clish, B. Hodgson, B. Dobson. Front row: J. Saiger, B. Chilsholm, W. Nichol, D. Cowan, T. Carter.

A Wheatley Hill Cricket Team in the 1940s. The photograph includes: George Allison, Bill Marshall, Harold Simpson, Tommy Clish, Jackey Jordan, Eric Simpson, Derek Alderton, Sid Wilson, Joe Soulsby.

Wheatley Hill Orchestra in the 1920s. The orchestra was conducted by Mr Bob Walker and they played in churches and chapels throughout the district. Teddy Cain, a well-known figure in Wheatley Hill, played the violin in this orchestra.

Rosy Rapids Ladies Football Team, Wheatley Hill, 1909. Ladies football before the First World War was rare, as can be seen by their request for teams to play them on the photograph, 'engagements wanted'. Left to right: Meggy Lowther, Lizzy Luke, -?-, Meggy Farrow, Lizzy Champley, Meggy Philips, Bella Cowie (kneeling).

Each year the Lodge provided a sports day in the village for the children. This consisted of a parade through the village with children dressing up, and games, etc., being held, with prizes. In later years each child whose father worked at the colliery was eligible for a bag of sweets. This carnival was held in 1932 and shows the Carnival Queen – Gladys Dixon and her attendants – Gladys Metcalfe, Jane Topper, Elizabeth Humes and Josephine Astle. The picture was taken outside the Colliery Hotel, Lynn Terrace.

Sports day scene in 1962. The gentleman in the centre of the image is Mr Alderson, a teacher at the primary school for many years.

Louisa Street, Wheatley Hill. One might get the impression that the photograph is distorted in some way. This is not the case. This is how the colliery cottages in Wheatley Hill looked when built on sloping land. Louisa Street was above the railway line and was one of eight parallel rows.

This is the back of Maria Street, near Louisa Street. This view shows Wolmerhausen Street in the background. The roads at the front and rear of these houses were unmade.

Above: Railway carriages used as housing in Black Road, Wheatley Hill. These houses were used during the 1920s and were situated behind The Royalty Cinema. In an article in the *Durham Advertiser* in February 1927, the inhabitants of the carriages were referred to as 'Hut Dwellers' and were taken to court by Easington Rural District Council who issued an order requiring the owners to cease occupying them. In one case a woman who said she had six children told the court that after the death of her husband she sold her furniture and bought a railway carriage at Wheatley Hill. The Hut Dwellers were given until April 1927 to find other suitable accommodation. If other accommodation had not been found then the dwellers were to be charged 2/6 for every day they remained in the carriage accommodation.

Opposite below: Opening of the Aged Miners' Homes, 1925. These dwellings were built as a mark of remembrance to those from the village who fell in the First World War. Dignitaries at the opening ceremony were, back row, left to right: E. Luke, R. Barron, E. Cain, W. Rutherford, Dr Grant, J. Brown, J. Adair, C. Raffle, G. Buxton. Second row: G. Cowell, R. Moore, C. Bentham, W. Evans, T.S. Parkinson, M. Lamb. Third row: Chief Constable Morley, Inspector Bennett, R. Hird, J. Wetherell, H. Taylor, W. Potts, F. Quin, J. Welsh (architect), T. Taylor, J. Gilliland, M. Barrass JP. Front row: T. Parry, Miss Morley, Mrs Grant, G. Rhymer, Mrs Rhymer,, J. Howe, J. Hedley, J. Charlton.

Right: Invitation to the opening ceremony of Aged Miners' Cottages, 1925.

Below: East View, Wheatley Hill was also known locally as the 'Scheme Houses', which was the name given to these houses which made it possible for a miner to buy his own home. The owners of the colliery, The Weardale Steel, Coal and Coke Co., operated an 'easy purchase scheme' whereby workers at the pit could pay a deposit and have the remainder of the cost of the house deducted from his wages over fourteen years, when the property became his. House ownership for miners would have been almost impossible without the benefit of this scheme.

Wheatley Hill

Aged Mineworkers' Association.

The Committee of the above request the pleasure of your Company at the

OPENING CEREMONY

of

Twelve Aged Mineworkers' Cottages,
One Caretaker's House,
and Single Men's Hostel,
to be held in

Cemetery Road, Wheatley Hill,

on

Saturday, October 3rd, 1925.

Chair to be taken at 2 p.m. by

M. Barrass, Esq., J.P.,

When the Homes will be opened and the Keys presented to the People by

Mrs. G. Rhymer, Spennymoor.

Cemetery Road, Wheatley Hill. 10563

Wheatley Hill Isolation Hospital was built as a smallpox hospital with two wards, but as a smallpox hospital, the building was grossly underused. This made it unpopular with Durham County Council who as early as 1914 labelled it a white elephant, and wanted to change its use to a sanatorium for consumption patients as they felt it unlikely that the area would suffer from an epidemic of smallpox owing to the increased number of smallpox vaccinations available. This led to the decision, in 1953, to sell the hospital and surrounding land.

Thornley station, Wheatley Hill which was situated at what is now known as Thornley Crossings which is nearer to Shotton Colliery than Thornley. There was much campaigning for the station to be relocated nearer Thornley during the late nineteenth and early twentieth centuries but it never came about.

two

Thornley

No.1 and Smokey Shaft, Thornley Pit in approximately 1890. This shaft was made into the upcast shaft when the new pit was sunk in 1905.

Mr John Edward Moore, aged forty-four, (standing on the right of kibble), formerly of Cassop and foreman sinker for Mr Johnson of East Bolden. This was the team that was responsible for sinking the No. 2 Shaft at Thornley in 1905.

Miners at Thornley Colliery (Harris, Fulcher, Cowell, Richard Peters, Corbett), *c.* 1955.

An early image of School Square, Thornley.

School Square, Thornley after renovations.

A picture postcard dated 1928 showing the new Thornley Pit. On the left are two rows of miners' cottages: Swinburne Street and Park Street. In the background and behind the water towers is High Street. The road shown in the foreground was the main road from Trimdon to Ludworth during the 1800s.

On the left of this image is the first Workmen's Club, opened in September 1900, and above is the Station Hotel. In 1920 a new hall was opened upstairs in the Workmen's Club.

The Barrel of Grapes public house, 1920. The public house was referred to locally as The Halfway House. After extensive renovations in the 1980s the pub is now called The Crossways Hotel and a few years ago it provided overnight accommodation for Prince William when his school visited the area on a geography field trip.

Three Horse Shoes, Thornley, on the right, with Hanley's butchers on the left, in Hartlepool Street. Bow Street chapel can be seen in the background on the right.

Albert Street, Thornley in 1910. This street was formerly known as Princess Street. The fish shop and the Dun Cow public house were on the right, whilst on the left there were three public houses: the King's Head, the Robin Hood and Binks' Vault (named after a local brewer and farmer, W. Binks).

Thornley Hall Farm. The old hall was demolished in 1600 and this is the replacement which still stands (and is occupied) today. This farm has a colourful history and was the home of the Roman Catholic Trollop family and the Spearmans. The farm has been in the hands of the Robinson family since 1937.

Gore Hill Farm, Thornley. This image was taken in the 1920s. Before mains water was available in Thornley, water had to be carried from a well at this farm. If a woman was unable to carry the water, the farmer would deliver for half a penny a bucket.

This is known locally as The Hillies or Hilly Howly. It is also known by some as 'the beauty spot' for its rural nature was in stark contrast to the coal-mining areas of Wheatley Hill and Thornley. The Thornley cricket team played their games on a field here from the 1930s until the 1950s.

Hartlepool Street South, Thornley, in about 1920. The image shows Ashford's butchers, The Good Intent public house, Scott's shop and the Roman Catholic church. The wording on the photograph says: 'When you see Thornley like this, you're drunk my boy, you're drunk.' The Barnett family took over the butcher's shop in 1928.

The water tanks which provided the village with water during the 1950s. The top tank was to feed the colliery manager's house and the top of the village. The bottom tanks fed the bottom of the village. The tanks were situated behind High Street, which was known earlier as Quarry Street.

Thornlaw Bank, Thornley. 7059

Thornlaw North, Thornley, council-owned housing built in the mid-1920s at a cost of £750 per house. These houses were known locally as 'the gray houses'.

The opening of Dunelm Road, Thornley, a successful colliery housing scheme which opened in August 1924. The scheme involved the building of 125 houses by the Weardale Steel, Coal and Coke Co. which were bought by workmen at the colliery at a rate of 7s per week (which was deducted from their wages). The scheme made it possible for colliery workers to own their own property, a situation that would have been unlikely without this arrangement.

Thornley 'Over 60s' in the 1950s. This image shows Alf Dobbin (on the left) and Mrs Bullock (sixth left) in the middle row. Front row: Mrs Kilbourn (first on the left), Mr Pattison (fourth left) and Mrs Lowes (second right).

Thornley Aged Miners' Homes, The Villas, were opened on Saturday 14 November 1914 by Mrs G. Curry. The land that the houses were built on cost £350 and the twelve houses £1,998. Accommodation for eight single men was also made available by the manager of the pit, Mr George Curry, Dr John Wilson, MP and the Dean of Durham, Dr Hensley Henson.

Post Office Street, Thornley (on the right). School Square can be seen at the rear. The white cottages are Pit Street and behind is Dyke Street and Quarry Street. In 1919 Post Office Street was one of the streets that were altered from single-storey housing to two-storey. When the structural changes were complete, the streets changed their names also – Pit Street became Pitt Street, whilst Stable Street, Post Office Street and Quarry Street lost their old names and were renamed High Street.

Austin 21 hearse which was first registered in 1928. It was used by Mr T. W. Kirk of Thornley until 1950 and remained in storage until 1970. The hearse is mounted on a basic Austin 20 chassis powered by a 24.5HP six-cylinder side-valve engine. The coachwork was built by Slater, a Nottingham company. Of particular interest are the cut-glass windows and the plush finished interior. The hearse is in the Beamish Museum and is still in full working order.

The Hippodrome Theatre, Thornley opened in September 1912. The hall could accommodate 1,000 people, 400 each in the pit and stalls and 200 in the overhead circle. The building was provided with five fire exits and, for additional safety, a fireproofed ceiling.

Young's newsagents, Hartlepool Street, still a newsagent's shop run by G.W. Barrett.

Thornley Women's Section of the Royal British Legion in 1966 with a cup awarded for the greatest increase in membership. Standing, from left to right: Jennie Burnham, Bettie Atkin, Brenda Coxon, Brenda Vassey, Mrs Redshaw, Mrs Langley. Front row: Mrs ?, Lizzie Clark and her granddaughter Yvonne Atkin.

Thornley Roman Catholic School, Infants Class 2 and 3, 1950. Back row, left to right: Phil Edwards, Don O'Connor, Peter Hepple, John Carr, Barry Millan, Andrew Bonar, Jimmy Hoban, Malcolm Williams, Jimmy Richardson, Paul Luke. Front row: Michael English, Ena Ramshaw, Joan Gorman, Ann Dryden, Eileen Bruce, Monica Maughan, Laura Philips, Ian Bell.

Thornley Junior and Infants School before 1900. The teacher is Miss Hill, who became head mistress of the Junior Mixed School in 1900. Miss Hill, originally from Scotland, retired in 1927.

Thornley Junior and Infants School. The foundation stone was laid in 1876 for a school to provide accommodation for 600 children in Thornley. The school was built in Cooper's Terrace and cost £3,721.

J.T. Scott & Sons' department store in Hartlepool Street, Thornley in the 1950s. Most people did at least some of their shopping in this store as it offered a credit arrangement.

Hartlepool Street, Thornley again in the 1950s. This image shows Stan Cook's fruit and vegetable shop and, on the far right, Ted Wilson's gents hairdressers.

Elliott's General Dealers situated in Hartlepool Street, Thornley in the 1940s. This shop was eventually taken over by Whitfield's chemists. The Durham District Services bus timetable can be seen on the wall to the left of the shop window.

Kirk's General Dealers, Hartlepool Street, *c.* 1910.

Opposite below: Hartlepool Street, Thornley, *c.* 1910. This shows Hanley's butchers, the Three Horse Shoes public house and the Thornley branch of the Station Town & District Co-operative Wholesale Society, known locally as 'The Store'.

Vesting Day, outside Thornley Colliery, 1 January 1947. This celebration by the colliery band was to acknowledge the coal mines being nationalised – out of the hands of private enterprise and into the hands of the Government. This was a great day for the miners – they really felt that nationalisation would solve their problems with regard to their work in the pits.

This is July 1992 and the last time that Thornley Colliery Band and banner paraded through Thornley on its way to the annual Durham Miners' Gala.

Thornley Colliery Band in 1929 in the pit yard. This photo was taken prior to the band travelling to the Crystal Palace Brass Band Contest, which they won. The band were rewarded with £7 in cash and a new trombone, which cost seven guineas. Mr Edward Kitto was their conductor at this time.

The old cricket pavilion at The Hilly cricket pitch. In the foreground is the roller that rolled the wicket.

Cricket match in The Hilly. Matches used to take place on this pitch on most Saturday and Sunday afternoons during the cricket season.

Thornley Colliery Mechanics Football Team during the 1960s. Front row (left to right): Lenny Perry, Gordon Abbs, Ernie Porter, Dave Robson. Back row: Alf Abbs, John Davies, Eddie Wilkinson, - ? -, George Armstrong, Stan Dower.

Village sports day. The day comprised of a fancy dress parade, decorated horse and cart floats, the colliery band and banner marching through the village and sports held on the show field behind Garden Terrace. This photograph shows a 'Runaway Wedding to Gretna Green'.

Remembrance Day 1958 at Thornley war memorial, Hartlepool Street. Left to right: Hilda Slater, Nurse Hannah Brewster, Rowland Brewster and Bob Slater. On Saturday 23 May 1959 a new war memorial was unveiled and dedicated at Thornley. The new memorial replaced the First World War memorial that was destroyed in a fire at the Miners' Welfare Institute in 1944.

Quarry Street, Thornley. The bottom street is Church Street.

St Bartholomew's church, Thornley was consecrated in August 1843 by the Bishop of Durham.

Procession to mark the opening of St Godric's School, Thornley Road, in 1908.

St Godric's RC School, Thornley Road, which opened in 1908.

Thornley police station. Pictured at the door is Sgt Thomas Samson, who was stationed at Thornley from 1870 to 1900.

A 1960s view of Thornley Pit. This photograph was taken from No. 2 Pit pulleys of the colliery yard, offices, store house and washery. The view also includes Thornley police station, Colliery Inn, the village clock and the white gable end of the Edinburgh Arms.

Above: A serious fire broke out at Thornley Colliery at 9 p.m. on Saturday night on the 8 May 1875. The fire caused extensive damage to the heapstead buildings but without fatal results. The damage was estimated at £20,000. This early image, taken soon after the fire, shows the devastation caused to Thornley Colliery.

Right: Closure of Thornley Pit and the felling of the Pit Chimney, 1972.

The Villas, Thornley. Good quality private housing, probably built for occupation by mangers at the Thornley Pit.

Cooper's Terrace, Thornley in 1910, at the top of the bank. Theodore Cottage is on the left. These miners' cottages had no running water or electricity. Mr Les Burlison lived in No. 3 Cooper's Terrace and ran a shop from his house.

The rear of Cooper's Terrace during the 1920s. The standpipe is where all the residents of the street obtained their water.

The Villas, Thornley. The house on the left, covered with ivy, was Dr Todd's house and surgery for many years. He carried out operations there.

An earlier image of The Villas, Thornley, looking in the opposite direction. There is no ivy on the house occupied by Dr Todd. The house next to the doctor's was the Presbytery for Roman Catholic priests which is today the Catholic Club.

Dunelm Road, Thornley – private housing. On the left is the Station Town Co-operative store.

This photograph was taken during the 1950s in Asquith Street, Thornley and shows Baldasera's ice-cream cart.

High Street, Thornley, 1960s. The image shows The Colliery Inn on the left and colliery workshops on the right.

Above: The Railway Tavern, Chapel Street, Thornley, formerly the Engine Tavern. Bob Dawson is standing on the corner. The pub was known locally as 'Ginger Dawson's' and is said to have had the best pint of beer in Thornley.

Left: The Station Hotel, Hartlepool Street, Thornley was opposite the Workmen's Club. Unfortunately, this is the only image available.

Opposite above: Thornley Workmen's Club, Hartlepool Street. This image was probably taken in 1912, eight years after the club opened in August 1904.

Opposite below: The Halfway House (Barrel of Grapes) in the 1960s. The image also shows the Thornley Dog Track.

WORKMEN'S CLUB THORNLEY

Law. Thornley

Thornley post office, Hartlepool Street in the 1920s. This image shows Miss Gull on the left.

Hartlepool Street, 1910.

Thornley Pit Head Baths opened in January 1933. The baths cost £18,000 and could accommodate 1,500 men. For the first time each workman had a separate locker for clean clothes and pit clothes.

Hartlepool Street in 1919, showing G. Ashford's shop on the left. The pub receiving a delivery could be The Black Bull.

Ashford's butchers, Hartlepool Street, before 1928. Also shown is the Good Intent public house, Scott's shop and the Catholic Rooms.

Kirk's general dealers. Hartlepool Street, Thornley in approximately 1920.

three

Wingate

View of Wingate Grange Pit. This colliery was first opened by Lord Howden and Partners in 1839. Ownership by the lord gave rise to shafts known as the Lord and Lady shaft. The pit later became the property of John Gully (1860s) and The Wingate Coal Co. (1880s). The pit contained the following seams, varying in thickness from 2ft 10in. to 5ft 2in. and at depths ranging from 80 to 147 fathoms: the Five Quarter, the Main, Low Main, Hutton, Harvey, and the Busty. The pit provided employment to all men and boys in Wingate in its heyday. The coal from Wingate was shipped at Hartlepool, and was known on the London Coal Exchange as the 'Caradoc', a previous name of Lord Howden.

The horses that were used to haul the coals on the surface at Wingate Grange Pit.

On 14 October 1906 at 11.40 p.m. an explosion occurred in Wingate Grange Pit and twenty-six men lost their lives. The photograph shows a funeral procession making its way to either Station Town or Hutton Henry Cemetery. The small horse-drawn carriage behind the hearse was for the wife or parents of the deceased. The houses in the background are in Station Lane which was the beginning of Station Town. The funeral route would be lined on both sides with people paying their respects, the men standing bare-headed.

A scene showing the crowds of people waiting for news of the Wingate Pit Disaster, 1906.

Another image of the 1906 explosion. This time it shows a body being brought out of the pit on a stretcher and taken to the joiner's shop where all the bodies were placed in coffins made by the colliery joiners.

A 1906 funeral procession for victims of the Wingate Grange explosion. This particular funeral was on its way to either Station Town or Hutton Henry Cemetery. The miners' lodge band is marching behind the banner.

Above: A further funeral for victims of the explosion in 1906. The hearse being used looks to have been provided by Tonks Hardware shop in Wingate. The procession is shown going through Station Town near to where the Corner House public house is today.

Right: The day the memorial was dedicated, 21 December 1907, to men and boys killed in the Wingate Explosion. The memorial was built with money raised by public subscription.

The memorial to the pit disaster. Cast-iron railings have been erected around the memorial. On the left of the image can be seen part of the school caretaker's house, then The Palace cinema. The shop facing it is Holcroft's wholesale fruiterers.

A view of Church Street on the right and the Wingate Board School on the left. The school was built in 1877 and the house next to it with the large chimney stack was built for the caretaker. The wall at the front right was the bottom of the garden of the bungalow, Ruby Cottage, built for the colliery engineer. The building below the school was the literary institute where Peter Lee went to self-improvement night classes. On the left is the Colliery School, built in 1841.

The second shop down in this view of Church Street was Saddler Brown's. The horse and coop cart in the image would probably be taking a miner's coal allowance for delivery. The colliery disaster memorial is in the centre of the photograph. The Palace Cinema was opened in 1914.

This is Station Lane leading to Wingate Station, hence the name. The large house at the top eventually became the home of the manager of the Co-operative store. The road to the right led to Station Town, which gained its name from the houses built to house the miners at the Hutton Henry Pit. The nearest building to the new houses was Wingate Station and therefore the name of Station Town was formed. The engine and trucks going over the bridge would be taking coal from the Trimdons to Hartlepool.

Wingate Station was sited on the south side of the village. The station was on the Hartlepool to Ferryhill line. It was a fairly busy line with passenger trains and mineral trains using it for journeys and deliveries to Hartlepool.

The crossings, Wingate. This image shows the point at which the mineral line crossed the main road. The line ran from the colliery to join up with the Sunderland to Hartlepool line. The building on the left was a Methodist chapel which had a schoolroom.

The Level Crossing, Wingate.

Another view of the Crossings, Wingate. The building in the centre with the hipped roof was the office of John Wilson Hays, architect. The man in the foreground is Ted Hughes, Master Mason at the colliery.

Heath View was a street of houses adjacent to the road leading to Hutton Henry Colliery. Little is known about this pond but as shown, there was a model yacht club which must have been unusual in a colliery village at the time. The dress of the ladies suggests a date of around the 1920s.

North Road, Wingate leading to The Fir Tree. Note the white brick around the doors and windows. The houses are still there but there is no trace of this feature. The paling fence is long gone too but its foundations are still evident. The house on the left has a 'For Sale' sign up. I wonder what the asking price was?

Another shot of North Road, Wingate, with hens roaming in the street. The house with the greenhouse attached eventually became Weighall the Jeweller's. On the right, next to the tree stump is Moore Lane leading to Wellfield Farm. The grammar school was built here in 1911.

The Lane, Wingate. This photograph was taken prior to 1906. The Lane eventually became Salters Lane leading to the Fir Tree crossroads. The men sat at the roadside were probably miners passing the time of day.

Another image of The Lane taken north to south. This photograph was taken prior to 1906. The house with the two dormer windows eventually became Henry's Fish Shop.

This is the area below the railway crossing in Wingate. To the right is the Caradoc Arms (named after the Caradoc family, which was the original name of Lord Howden, the first owner of Wingate Grange Colliery). Also shown is the Victoria Inn. The building with the spire was The George and Dragon and on the right is The Railway Tavern.

Wingate Front Street in the early 1930s, showing Doggarts department store. Doggarts was a family-owned business, very popular throughout the district with mining families as a result of their 'clubs' which allowed people to pay weekly for purchases at the store.

Doggarts Store at a later date than the previous image. The smart exterior reflects the inside. Female staff wore a uniform of black skirts and white blouses and male staff wore a dark coloured suit. As well as Wingate, Doggarts had stores in Spennymoor, Chester-le-Street, Houghton-le-Spring, Bishop Auckland, Crook, Stockton, Billingham, Durham, Consett, Darlington, Gateshead, Seaham, Stanley, Ashington, Shildon and New Shildon with a Peterlee Branch opening in the 1960s to replace the Wingate branch when it closed.

This Doggarts' delivery van has been restored and is on show at a rally for vintage vehicles.

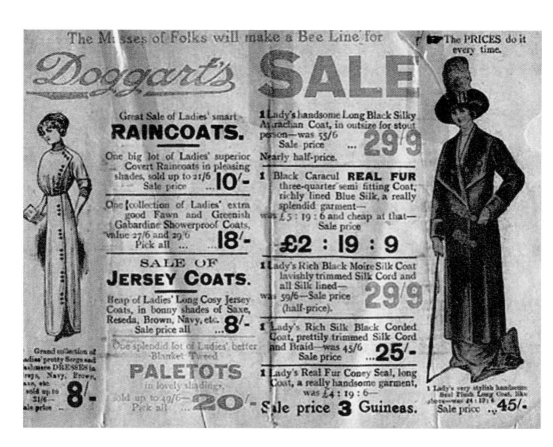

Above: This is a sale notice from Doggarts department store in 1902.

Left: Wingate Front Street under flood conditions. A beck ran from the colliery site and passed under the road behind where the bus is on this view and on to Headshope Dene. There had been a heavy downpour, and a flood in the front street was the result. The bus shown in the image is the G & B – a service run by Gillett & Baker from Quarrington Hill which ran between Durham and Hartlepool and Bishop Auckland. The buses were well known in the Durham area for their brown and cream livery.

Front Street, Wingate looking north. The clock shows 5.10 p.m. on a wet day. The variety of shops in the street is evident in the image. The shop with the bills on the gable end was the cobbler's and the road between that shop and the next led to Glass's brickyard.

Appleby's boot and shoe shop with a gold-coloured lady's boot hanging over the shop.

Stephenson's shop, which later became Victor Neilson's and later still, the local library. Its present-day use is as a tanning salon.

Opposite below: Front Street on a sunny day. The sun blinds out are over shop windows – a sight not often seen these days.

Right: Walter Willson's grocery shop, Front Street, one of two shops owned by the same company in Wingate. This image shows a rebuilt store, the previous one having been burned to the ground. There were living quarters above this shop.

Below: Another image showing Walter Willson's grocery store at the bottom of Wingate Front Street, this time with staff standing outside. The door on the left would have led to the living quarters. Hams can be seen hanging in the shop doorway.

Above: Duncan's grocery store in Front Street, one of five grocers in the village. Next door to Duncan's is Mervyn Hodgson's, which sold electrical goods.

Left: This image, from the 1960s, shows the inside of Duncan's grocery shop. The assistants shown here are Miss West and Miss Longstaff and the photograph dates from the 1960s.

Opposite below: Wingate Lane Ends, which is now known as the Fir Tree crossroads. The road to the left was the main Durham to Hartlepool Road and went to Wheatley Hill. The road to the right was Wellfield Road and went to Castle Eden. The road straight ahead was Haswell Road and went to Shotton Colliery. The house on the right is Fir Tree Farm and on the left is the Fir Tree public house.

This image shows the Fir Tree House, which at the time of the photograph was run by J.J. Cowley, and the gentleman with the horse could be Mr Cowley.

Another image of The Fir Tree public house.

Fir Tree Garage recorded at a time when the area was undeveloped, *c.* 1919.

An image of the Fir Tree Garage in the early 1960s. The Pack Brothers owned the garage at this time. The tyre gantry can still be seen on this image and the previous one.

An Away Day.

A party of holiday makers at Blackpool. In the photograph are Mrs Proudlock, daughter Enid and Betty Unsworth.

Station Town Horticultural Club on a day out at York. The two villages of Wingate and Station Town, although joined, had their own allotment sites. There was a one hundred percent take-up for allotment gardens. Keen rivalry existed between the members and it was everyone's ambition to grow the best vegetables for the annual shows.

A schoolboy football team, 1911. The goalkeeper is wearing the obligatory flat cap. The boy in the back row on the left has a different shirt while the boy on the left at the front is wearing trousers. No funds for football strips!

Wingate Football Club 1935/36. Left to right, back row: H. Clogg (treasurer), D. Robinson, H. Walker, E. Thompson, M. Boulton (capt.), G. Lennard, J. Halsall, W. Flowers, F. Rickard. Front row: R. Champley (trainer), J. Holloday, R. Kyle, E. Smith, J. Bean, W. Slater.

Above: Wingate football team 1918/19.

Below: Wingate Sports Club football team 1930–1940. This was one of many teams that existed in the village. This image shows (left to right) back row: Dunn, Stones, Stones, Moyle, Watson, Russell. Front row: Harland, Dakin, Kaye, Bryson, Holcroft.

Wingate St Mary's football team. The photograph was taken at the Victoria ground, the home of Hartlepool United, to celebrate a cup final the team were in. The photograph includes: Tom Lenehan (manager), The Nevins Brothers, Hugh Teasdale, Tom Flanagan, John Hennessey and Peter Mason.

This multi-view postcard of Wingate shows A.J. Dawson Grammar School, the park bowling green (with tennis courts in the background), Salters Lane and the footbridge going over the stream that ran through the park. In the centre of the card is Wingate Grange Colliery which provided employment for most men in the village at the time the photograph was taken.

This image was taken outside The George and Dragon public house and looks like a celebration of a coronation or something similar. The older men who are bare-headed have a style of haircut popular in the day. The hair left after a short back and sides cut was brushed over to one side and called a 'tar brush'. The photograph was probably taken in the 1920s.

Christmas in the bar of The George and Dragon public house. The barmaid with the lace collar is Rose Thirlaway. Lighting was via paraffin lights suspended from the ceiling which would give a dim glow to the pub.

In 1841 a pit was sunk at South Wingate. It was initially known as Rodridge but came to be known as South Wingate at a later date. However both the colliery and the area became known locally as Hart Bushes. The Roadside Inn was at the bottom of the bank at South Wingate.

A group of miners outside the lamp cabin ready to go down the pit. The man on the left on the front row seems to have his knee pads already on under his trousers, as do some of the others. A common practice was for the miners to hang their knee pads on their belts until they were needed.

Another group of miners at the lamp cabin, ready with their lamps lit. The miner second from the right on the back row was Septimus Ord.

Opposite below: The Working Committee of the Wingate and Station Town Child Welfare. Left to right, back row: –?–, Mrs Grieves, Mrs M. Scott, Nurse Roberts. Front row: –?–, Nurse de Curry, –?–, Dr Willie Arthur.

Right: Dr Arthur was a general practitioner in Wingate for many years and is seen here in his study. The doctor kept a record of notable events in Wingate.

Below: Wingate Boys School. Only the boy in the centre middle row and the boy second left on the front row are wearing ties.

A.J. Dawson Grammar School, Wellfield Road, Wingate, 1954. The school had a wide catchment area and had a reputation for providing an excellent education.

A.J. Dawson School in Wellfield Road, Wingate was named after the Durham County educationalist. The grammar school offered the children of miners and other working-class families a marvellous opportunity to study to a high level and make university entrance possible. This image shows the junior choir in 1950/51: From the left, back row: (1) Harry Kellett, (2) Brian Harrison, (7) Eddie Gratton. Middle row: (3) June Legg, (4) Enid Roscamp, (6) Jean Oswald, (7) Rita Osbaldestin, (8) Dorothy ?. Front row: (2) Lettice Shenton, (4) Brenda Rowell, (6) Janet Stewart.

Wingate Council Junior School, Standard 1, seen in 1920. The boy fourth from the left on the back row is Bob Kyle and on his left is Mick Hockaday.

Wingate Junior School, *c.* 1975. The teacher is Mr Joss. The junior mixed school was built in 1911 and is situated in Moor Lane.

Wingate St Mary's RC School, Standards 3 and 4, 1909. This school was situated on land next to where the welfare park was to be built, and was a mixed school with pupils from five to fourteen years of age. There were five classrooms with an open fire in each room.

Wingate Wanderers 1956/57. The team was managed for ten years by Ron Gregson (shown on the far left). Ron kept a record of every player over these years, how many games they played, and how many goals each player scored. The player in the front row, third from the right, is Tom Flanagan, a prolific goal scorer.

A group of Wingate
pigeon fanciers
at a loft (note its
construction!). The
man in the back
row, second from
the left, seems to
be holding a watch.
Pigeon racing was
popular throughout
County Durham
with the miners and
they entered their
birds in races such as
'milers', 'inland' and
'over the water'.

A local Leek Club show with members watching the judging. Rivalry was keen in this competition and prizes were mostly household goods, some of which can be seen in the background – an ironing board, a fireside rug and an ottoman.

This is an image of The Salvation Army marching at the rear of The George and Dragon public house which is identifiable on the right by its spire, and Market Crescent on the left. The tall building on the left was the Colliers Arms which had been turned into flats at the time this image was taken, probably in the 1940s. The site of The George and Dragon is now the doctor's surgery and Lloyds Pharmacy.

Wellfield Road ran from the Fir Tree crossroads down to Castle Eden. This was the main road between Hartlepool and Durham City. The houses on the right were all private and on the left was the A.J. Dawson Grammar School. Judging by the car, a Morris Oxford or Austin Cambridge, the image was taken in the mid-1960s.

Wellfield Station.

An aerial view of the Wellfield area of Wingate.

Above: Wingate Transport collecting coal from the colliery.

Left: Wingate Jazz Band in 1921.

four

Ludworth

Left: Ludworth Tower, a Civic Trust Grade II listed monument. The tower stands near a rivulet and is a massive square structure of rude masonry believed to have been built in 1425. In the lower portion it contained a vaulted dungeon and above this an upper chamber, lighted by a few casements. In 1890 a large portion of this interesting relic of antiquity fell, leaving only the western wall standing.

Below: Ludworth Colliery was owned first by the Thornley Coal Co. which was taken over in 1886 by The Weardale Steel, Coal and Coke Co. Ludworth pit opened in about 1844/45 at a cost of £80,000.

Opposite above: Workers at Ludworth Colliery, 1924. The photograph includes, back row: assistant engineer, blacksmith, shaftman, locomotive driver. Front row: assistant blacksmith, three shaftmen, boilerman, electrician.

Opposite below: Resinking of the Ludworth shaft from the main coal seam in the Low Hutton Seam.

Left: Sale notice for Ludworth Colliery, 1871. The owners of the colliery, the Hartlepool Collieries Co., were in significant debt at the beginning of the 1870s and felt the only way they could continue mining at their other two collieries, Thornley and Wheatley Hill, was to sell the Ludworth Colliery site. Ludworth coal, along with that of Thornley and Wheatley Hill, was very good quality and sold on the London Coal Market as 'Thornley Wallsend'.

Below: Aerial view of Ludworth during the 1960s. North View shows the three public houses: the Ludworth Inn, the Queen's Head and the Standish Arms as a house. Also in the photograph, next door to the Standish Arms, is Ludworth post office. Margaret Street is to the left of North View.

The Standish Arms, Ludworth, named after the owner of the Ludworth Estate, W.S.C. Standish, and referred to locally as 'The Bottom House' or, before the First World War, 'Polly Vasey's' after the wife of the landlord, John George Vasey.

The Queen's Head, Ludworth was known locally as 'The Middle House'. The landlord in 1901 was John Grey.

The Ludworth Inn, known locally as 'The Top House'. This public house was often the venue for inquests carried out in the village for men who had been killed in the pit. The landlord in 1901 was Robert Champley.

Ludworth AFC, winners of the Haswell & District Football League Championship in 1909. The team were each presented with a gold medal with an enamelled centre at a ceremony in the village. The team was: Joseph Wilson (captain), J. Embleton, Sam Jones, Wilson Atkin, John Townsend, James Gutteridge, James Simpson, T. Craggs, M. Broderick, H. Errington, R. Cowey, George Bond, John Bond, Robert Holder and John Cook. The team's officials also appear in the photograph.

Ludworth football team 1927/28 were winners of the Wheatley Hill Aged Miners' Cup. In the first season of this football cup Ludworth beat Murton 5–3. Back row: W. Shutt (sec.), G. Briggs, ? Kitson, ? Laverick, T. Summers, M. Hagan (trainer). Middle row: O. Buck, J. Oxenham, W. Millar. Front row: T. Millar, J. Purvis, H. Hall, N. Soppitt, W. Soppitt.

An aerial view of Ludworth showing the old school in the background and the new school in the foreground, 1960s.

Ludworth school children, 1912. Second row from back: ? Hughes, -?-, ? Middlemass, Joe Grey, -?-, Lily Maitland, Sally ?, Mary ?. Front row: Bella Jopling, Frances Johnson, Lucy Jones, Lizzie Lister, Lizzie Hartley, -?-, Lizzie Greener. Front row: Joe Hartley, -?-, ? Simpson.

Ludworth School, 1914.

Ludworth School Infants Class 2, 1949.

Ludworth Women's Institute, 1950s.

Ludworth Women's Institute outing, 1950s.

Ludworth old people's party in the 1960s.

Shopping list of John Davison, farmer at Tower Farm, Ludworth, March 1882. The items were bought at Tonks' hardware shop, Wingate.

A drawing by the late Bob Lofthouse, a well-known naturalist from Ludworth. Bob loved animals, birds and nature in general and had a huge collection of stuffed birds and drawings such as this one in his home. Whilst fighting in the First World War, Private Lofthouse often wrote home about the wildlife he had seen whilst in the trenches. His collection was presented to Durham University upon his death.

Members of the Ludworth British Legion.

The little boy on the horse is Robbie Redfern and he is with his grandfather. The houses in the background are Mary Street, Ludworth, referred to locally as The Cottages. This image is likely to have been taken in the 1930s.

This photograph shows the old Ludworth School and St Andrew's Mission church in the background. It was probably taken in the 1950s.

Moor Crescent, Ludworth, council-owned housing.

Other local titles published by Tempus

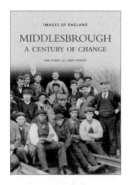

Middlesbrough: A Century of Change
IAN STUBBS AND JENNY PARKER

This splendid selection of over 270 old photographs of Middlesbrough illustrates some of the many changes that have occurred in town over the twentieth century. Compiled by two professionals of the libraries and museums service and endorsed by 'Middlesbrough Moving Forward', these images of streets, transport, industries and churches show exactly how far this enterprising Victorian town has come.

978 0 7524 3720 0

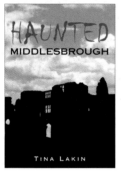

Haunted Middlesbrough
TINA LAKIN

'Remember that you have to believe to see,' writes the compiler of this chilling collection of stories. Telling of the inexplicable apparitions, manifestations, strange sightings and happenings remembered by Middlesbrough residents, this book is strongly recommended for anyone with an interest in the untold, paranormal heritage of the town.

978 0 7524 4193 1

Around Redcar
SHEILA BARKER

This selection of over 220 archive photographs illustrates some of the changes and events that have taken place in and around Redcar over the last century. The book also includes old images from the neighbouring communities of Coatham and Warrenby and recalls the life and times of local people at work and play throughout the area.

978 0 7524 3704 0

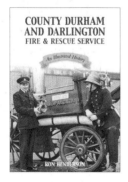

County Durham Fire and Rescue Service
RON HENDERSON

The County Durham and Darlington Fire and Rescue Service is responsible for protecting a population of just over half a million people, and the population of County Durham is reliant on the professionalism of the fire service in times of emergency. With this unique collection, featuring over 150 archive and modern photographs, fire historian Ron Henderson has created an evocative record detailing the post-war history of the fire service, beginning with its inception in 1948 up to the present day.

978 0 7524 4179 5

If you are interested in purchasing other books published by Tempus, or in case you have difficulty finding any Tempus books in your local bookshop, you can also place orders directly through our website

www.tempus-publishing.com